Native Americans
Who Inspire Us

By Analiza Quiroz Wolf

with Bryson Quiroz Wolf

Illustrated by Andreea Chele

TABLE OF CONTENTS

Jim Thorpe 6

Wilma Mankiller 14

Wes Studi 20

Elizabeth Peratrovich 26

John Herrington 32

Hattie Kauffman 38

Sitting Bull 44

Ryneldi Becenti 50

Allan Houser 56

Susan La Flesche Picotte 62

Jason Baldes 68

Maria Tallchief 74

Chester Nez 80

Mary Golda Ross 86

Cochise 92

Zitkala-Sa 98

Further Reading 106

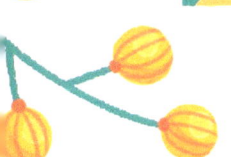

Native Americans come from many tribes and nations. There are 574 federally recognized tribes in the United States, each with their own unique customs, beliefs, and traditions. Whether Olympians, chiefs, Academy Award winners, or astronauts, they have shaped our history, our culture, and our world. Here are a few Native Americans who inspire us.

JIM THORPE

Sac and Fox Nation
1888 - 1953

Growing up on a farm, Jim loved to find a new adventure each day. He would run in the woods, run in the fields, and run anywhere his legs would take him.

When Jim was six, his family sent him to the nearest school, which was 23 miles away. Jim hated living away from his family. He hated being told what to do every moment of every day. He hated having to march in step to his classes, get his hair cut, wear a suit, and not have any free time. So, Jim turned to what he loved. He ran. He ran away from school all the way home.

Jim's family sent him to a school farther away. They thought this would stop Jim from running. Jim did not like the rules at his new school either, but there was one thing that he did like there – sports.

Jim noticed the high jumpers on the track team trying to clear the bar and failing. Jim asked if he could try. He wasn't dressed for sports and wore overalls and a work shirt. The boys laughed at him. Jim smiled, ran to the high bar, and easily jumped over it. It was his first try. He broke the school record!

The coach was amazed. He immediately asked Jim to try other track events. The coach had him try hurdles, hammer throw, and shot put. Jim had never tried any of these sports before, but he won over and over again. All those childhood years playing and doing what he loved set Jim up to be a natural athlete.

Jim asked to try football. The coach thought Jim was too small. Jim asked again and again. Finally, the coach gave Jim a chance. The coach spread the team out across the field and told Jim to try and get past all of them. Jim spun, swerved, and ran past the whole team – on his first try. The coach was amazed.

In 1907, at one of Jim's first football games, he helped his team beat the powerful University of Pennsylvania and became the star of the team. He didn't play just one position, he played four – running back, defensive back, placekicker, and punter. He could throw the football in a perfect spiral, dodge tacklers, and outrun even the quickest defenders. He was so fast he could even catch his own punt!

Jim led his football team to the college national championship. He was proud to show everyone that his team of Native Americans could win against the best schools in the country. He wanted to show the world what Native Americans could do, that they were just as good as anyone – if not better.

In 1912, Jim sailed to Sweden to compete in the Olympics. People from all over the world came for the games, and they came to see the famous Native American who had entered the pentathlon and decathlon. To win the pentathlon, Jim would have to best the other athletes in five difficult events — the long jump, javelin throw, sprint, discuss throw, and the 1,500-meter run (that's almost a mile). Jim had never competed in a pentathlon before.

Jim surprised the crowd and won the gold medal!

Jim continued to surprise the crowd and the world. Just a week later, Jim competed in the decathlon, twice as hard as the pentathlon. The competition lasted three days. It tested strength, speed, and endurance. The first day it poured rain. Jim splashed down the track in the 100-meter dash in 11.2 seconds – an Olympic record! This was not matched again until the Olympics 36 years later. On the second day, Jim's shoes were stolen. One teammate had an extra shoe that was too small. They found another shoe in a garbage can that was too big. It was just in time because Jim's turn at the high jump was about to start. He won! Later that afternoon, Jim competed in the 110-meter hurdles. He ran it in 15.6 seconds – again an Olympic record not matched until the Olympics 36 years later. On the final day of the competition, Jim competed in his favorite event, the almost one-mile race. Jim still wore his mismatched shoes – and won!

People were amazed. Jim not only won the decathlon, he set the world record! He was the first Native American to win not just one but two gold medals. Newspapers declared Jim the greatest athlete in the world.

Jim went on to play professional football and baseball, but he stayed humble. He was a gifted and talented athlete who stayed true to who he was: a Native American who loved being out in the open playing sports. He said, "I have always liked sport and only played or run races for the fun of the thing."

Jim inspires us to *do what we love* and to show the world what we can do.

WILMA MANKILLER

Cherokee
1945 - 2010

Wilma loved her big family. She had 10 brothers and sisters. They lived in a tiny house with no electricity. But they filled that house with love. They played together, hunted together, and grew their own food together – peanuts, strawberries, and more.

The government wanted Native American families like Wilma's to move to big cities. The government wanted Native Americans to forget their land and their culture. Wilma's family did not want to move, but they needed better jobs and better schools. So, just before Wilma turned 11, she and her family boarded a train from Oklahoma to San Francisco for a new life.

But Wilma's new life was not better. Other kids teased her. They made fun of her accent. They made fun of her clothes. Most of all, they made fun of her last name – Mankiller.

Wilma was sad and homesick. She missed her friends, but she wasn't the type of person who just stayed sad. Wilma found a place where she could feel better. It was a center that helped Native Americans connect with their people, history, and traditions. There, people looked like her. They understood her. They told her the name, Mankiller, meant village protector and had an important history that had been passed down through generations. Wilma felt proud of her name and decided to dedicate her life to living up to it. She wanted to be a village protector.

In 1969 when Wilma was 24, she found other village protectors who were standing up for Native Americans. Over a hundred Native Americans were occupying Alcatraz Island in San Francisco Bay. They wanted the U.S. government to return the island to Native Americans. They wanted to use the island as a Native American cultural center, and they refused to leave until the island was given back. Wilma saw her chance to be a village protector. She became a spokesperson and raised money to buy supplies like food and blankets for those involved in the occupation. The occupation lasted almost two years, but the government still refused to keep their promise of giving the land back to its people. Wilma was sad and angry. She did not think this was fair. She decided to be a village protector back home in Oklahoma and to serve her Cherokee community.

Wilma moved back to Oklahoma. She asked her community what they needed and learned they needed clean water. She remembered as a girl how her Cherokee community would depend on each other, often trading among themselves to get by. Maybe they could take care of this water problem by themselves too.

Wilma kicked off the Bell Waterline Project. She led 100 Bell, Oklahoma residents to build a 16-mile pipeline to bring clean water to their homes. After eight months, it was done. This inspired similar projects across the Cherokee nation.

Wilma wanted to help more people. She decided to run for deputy chief of her Cherokee tribe. But her own Cherokee people made fun of her. They thought a chief should be a man, not a woman. People threatened to hurt her, and the tires on her car were slashed. Wilma was scared and sad. She reminded herself that her goal was to be a village protector for her tribe. She refused to pull out of the race. She would honor her name.

Wilma became the first woman ever to be elected Cherokee Chief. She created jobs, homes, health clinics, and children's programs. She even got President Clinton to meet with her and other Native American leaders. The president promised to respect the tribes and allow them to make decisions for themselves. In 1998, President Clinton gave Wilma the Presidential Medal of Freedom. He celebrated Wilma as a leader who protected not only the rights of the Cherokees but all people in America.

Wilma inspires us to *be a village protector*, caring and helping others in our communities.

WES STUDI

Comanche
Born 1947

When Wes was a little boy, his favorite TV show was "The Lone Ranger." He and his friends would act out scenes from the show. Everyone wanted to be the Lone Ranger, but no one wanted to be the Lone Ranger's Native American friend, Tonto.

Wes asked his dad, "How does somebody get into the acting business?"

His dad said, "You have to be 6 feet tall and blond-haired and blue-eyed to be in movies."

Wes wasn't sure if his dad was joking. Then he saw a movie where the famous Apache warrior Geronimo was played by a white person with blonde hair and blue eyes – not by a Native American. Wes did not think this was fair!

Wes learned that there were other things that were not fair for Native Americans. When he and his friends went to a store, shopkeepers would watch them, sure they were going to steal something. People would look down on them and treat them like they were nothing. People would tell him that Native Americans were selfish and only cared about themselves.

Wes wanted to prove them wrong. He wanted to show that Native Americans were honest, worthy, and willing to put their lives on the line for their country. He decided to serve in the military. This was during the Vietnam War, and the Vietnam War was a scary place. Wes discovered how important taking care of his fellow soldiers was. They didn't care about the color of anyone's skin; they just cared about each other. They were all one team.

After the war, when Wes came home, he wanted to fight for the rights of his people. He was part of the Trail of Broken Treaties protest in 1972. The U.S. government had broken its treaty promises over and over again. Wes joined other Native Americans and marched to Washington D.C. to demand the government follow through on their promises.

After the march, Wes heard a movie director was looking for Native Americans to act in a movie called "Dances with Wolves." Wes remembered the many movies he'd watched where Native American roles were not played by Native Americans. He did not have much experience in acting, but he decided to try out. Many people competed for the part. But Wes got the job!

Wes worked hard and did his best. When he played the part of the tough Pawnee warrior, he played himself. He remembered how he felt when people looked down on him as a Native American. He remembered how he felt fighting during the Vietnam War. He remembered protesting so that the U.S. government would follow through on promises to the Native Americans. He felt angry and sad and ready to fight. He brought all of these feelings to his acting.

Wes did an amazing job. He acted in more movies such as, "The Last of the Mohicans" and "Geronimo." He even won an Academy Award. He was proud to be the first Native American to win one. He was proud to show that Native Americans can do anything.

With the spotlight on him, Wes became a voice for his people. In 2019, he helped create a film that exposed the lies people told about Native Americans. When the COVID-19 pandemic struck, Wes spoke up about its impact on Native Americans and raised money for food, water, and medical care.

Wes inspires us to *use our life experiences* to help us achieve our dreams.

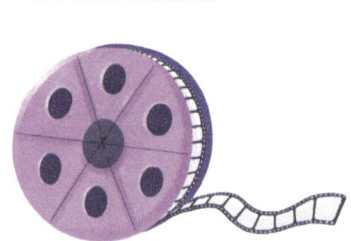

ELIZABETH PERATROVICH

Tlingit
1911 - 1958

As a girl, Elizabeth liked to listen to her father. Her dad was a Presbyterian minister, and she would travel with him around Alaska to different native villages as he shared stories about their religion. Elizabeth watched how he would speak and how people would pay attention.

To her Tlingit people, speaking was important. It was the way they shared stories about their culture and passed them on to their children.

When she started school, Elizabeth was surprised that none of her teachers were Native American and that speaking Tlingit was forbidden. She was also surprised there were no white students in her classes. White people had separate schools and better ones. They had separate hospitals, theaters, and restaurants, and those places were better too. Back then, it was legal to discriminate against Native Americans.

In 1924, the U.S. passed the Indian Citizenship Act. This was supposed to help Native Americans be treated more fairly. But it did not. When Elizabeth tried to shop at a store, she saw a sign, "No Dogs or Natives Allowed."

Elizabeth joined other Native Americans to fight for their rights. She was now married with three young children. Elizabeth convinced her husband to move to the territorial capital, Juneau, where they could talk to more leaders. Unfortunately, while looking for a place to live in Juneau, the owner said he could not rent to them because they were Native American.

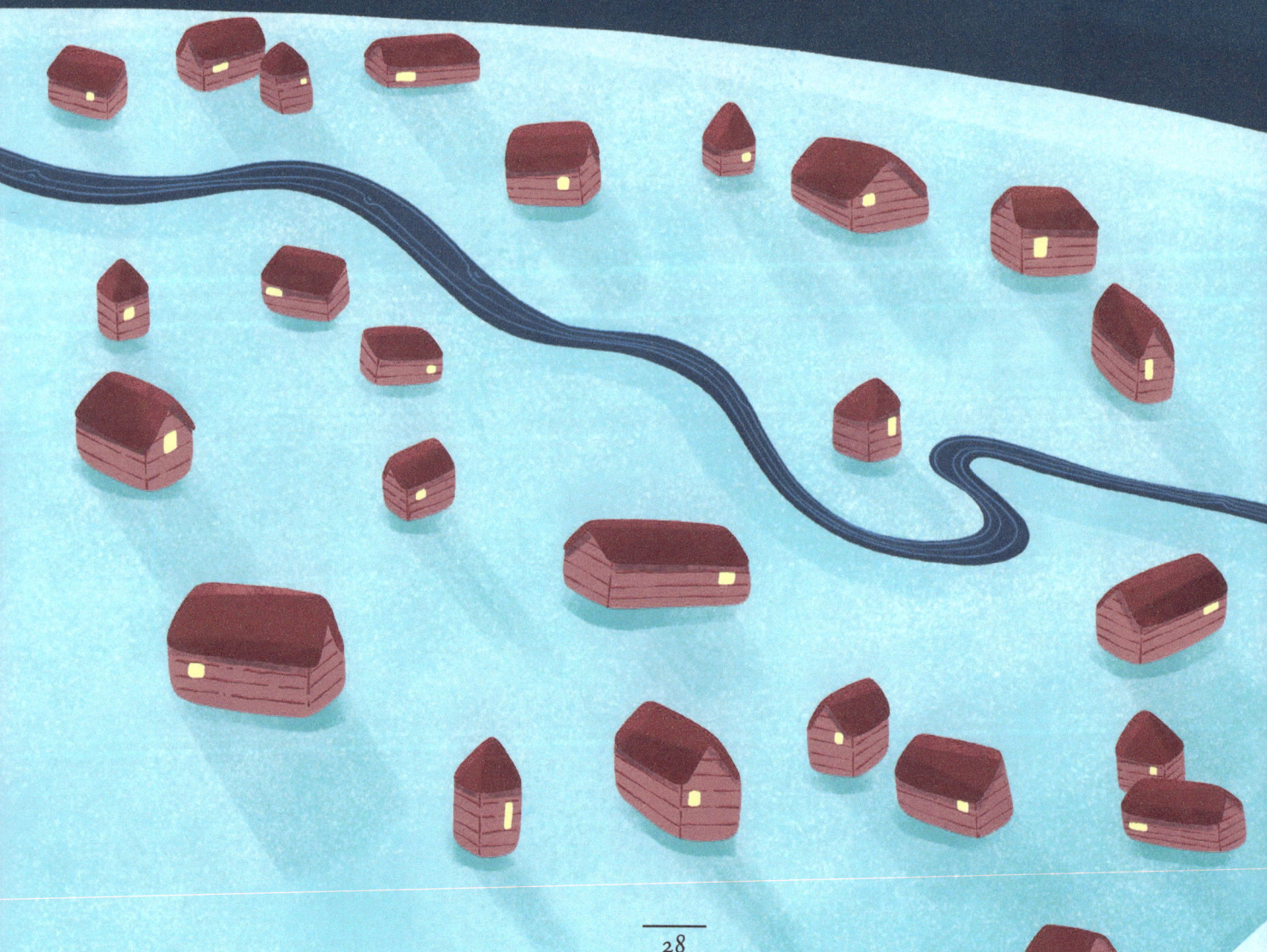

Although Alaska wasn't yet a state, it was a territory of the United States. It had a new governor who was Jewish and knew what it felt like to not be treated fairly. Elizabeth asked for his help, and he agreed. He told her that she needed to travel around Alaska telling people to vote for a new bill that would make things better – for everyone.

Just like her father, Elizabeth traveled around to many villages, talking and teaching and sharing stories. She even took a dog team to some remote villages.

When she met with fellow Native Americans, Elizabeth did it the Tlingit way. She shared stories, including how she was turned away from renting a home. She shared why this new bill would help stop unfair treatment like this for their people.

The big day came. It was 1945, and the Alaska lawmakers would vote on the Territory's Anti-Discrimination Act. The Territorial Legislature courthouse was crowded. After many speeches, it was Elizabeth's turn to speak. She faced the mostly white, mostly male, mostly unfriendly crowd. She was nervous. She remembered her dad and the power of his words. She remembered how important it was for Native Americans to be treated fairly.

Elizabeth took a deep breath. She spoke from the heart. She shared stories about what it was like to be treated as a second-class citizen, to be refused housing or access to a store because of the color of her skin.

There was a wild burst of applause. They won, and the law passed!

Alaska made history with the country's first anti-discrimination bill. Now Alaska Native Americans could learn, shop, be entertained, and be healed in the same places as whites. This didn't just help Alaska, it helped the entire country. Twenty years later, Martin Luther King Jr. led the battle for civil rights so that there was a law for the whole country for people to be treated fairly, no matter who they were.

Elizabeth shows us that *words matter*. One person speaking from the heart can create change.

JOHN HERRINGTON

Chickasaw Nation
Born 1958

When John was a boy, he watched on TV as the first people walked on the moon. He got so excited he made himself a cardboard box spaceship. When he sat in it, he imagined being shot to the moon. He dreamed of being an astronaut.

Sometimes John's dream seemed impossible. The astronauts on TV were not Native American like he was. No astronauts struggled in school like he did. No astronauts moved as much as he had. His family moved 14 times before he was 18 years old, so John never got to know his teachers well. No one explained to him why school was important, and he never felt inspired to learn. Even when he was in college, he wasn't inspired. John failed his classes and flunked out.

But John was good at rock climbing, and he found a job where he could climb cliffs in the Colorado mountains. Up high on the cliff, John would hold a mirror so light could reflect off of it. The survey crew at the bottom of the cliff would use that reflection to calculate how tall the mountain was. It was the first time John saw how math worked in the real world. It was the first time John learned why school was important.

Hanging from the cliff and looking into the sky, John remembered his astronaut dream. He knew all astronauts went to school, so he went back to college. John focused, studied, and got good grades.

He met a captain in the U.S. Navy who encouraged John to apply, so John joined the Navy. Astronauts went to a special test pilot school, so John went to test pilot school too. John learned how to fly different airplanes like the P-3 Orion and the de Havilland Dash 7. He wanted to have as much knowledge as possible to show he was ready to be an astronaut. When his chance came, John applied to be an astronaut. Thousands of people applied too. John was not chosen.

But John did not give up. He kept going to school, working hard, learning, and trying his best. John got a second chance. He applied and was chosen! John's hard work had paid off!

In 2002, John joined the crew of the Endeavour space shuttle and became the first Native American in space. Before the shuttle lifted off, there was a special ceremony of drumming, chants, and dancing from his Chickasaw Nation. John brought the Chickasaw flag, a purplish-blue flag with the seal of the Chickasaw Nation with him into space. He also brought an eagle feather for courage and a flute made by his Cherokee friend. John loved his time in space seeing the beautiful blues and greens of earth. But what he loved most was knowing that he had worked hard to make his dream come true.

When John landed back on Earth, he wanted to share his story with as many Native American children as possible. John decided to take a bike ride from Cape Flattery, Washington, to Cape Canaveral, Florida, and stop by reservations all along the way. John wanted to be the person he had needed as a child. He wanted to encourage Native American children to see why school was important and how they could make connections between what they learned in class to what they wanted to do in real life.

John teaches us that *it's OK to fail*. He inspires us to keep trying and go for our dreams.

HATTIE KAUFFMAN

Nez Perce
Born 1955

Hattie had six siblings, and they always took care of each other, which could be a challenge. Hattie's parents had challenges of their own, and they often left Hattie and her brothers and sisters alone. From the time Hattie was only four, she had to take her turn caring for the baby.

As she got older, sometimes that meant she had to stay home from school. Hattie would tell the baby many stories to keep them both entertained.

Hattie learned that she loved telling stories, and she was really good at it. Hattie's storytelling talent came in handy during her first year of college when she was 17 years old. Hattie was at a student meeting when someone walked in and said, "We want to let you students talk for five minutes on the radio."

No one raised their hand, so Hattie did. Hattie shared stories about what was happening at her college. She spoke clearly and well, and this opened the door to getting a job at her college's radio station!

Hattie was excited, but she had never written news stories before. Hattie listened and learned from other reporters and her reporting skills got better and better. Another door opened. She got a job on TV as a reporter and then as an anchor for KING 5 News in Seattle. That opened another door. She became a reporter on Good Morning America. Which opened another door.

In 1989, Hattie became the first Native American to report news to people across America.

Hattie was committed to telling her stories in a respectful and honest way. News reporters often ignored stories that featured Native Americans and the issues they cared about. When Native Americans were covered in the news, it was usually to show them protesting or dancing in traditional costumes with feathers in their hair. Hattie knew there were important stories about Native Americans, and she wanted to tell them.

At the time, a mystery illness was affecting young Navajos. TV stations called it the Navajo flu. Hattie was determined to tell a different version of the story. She made sure to explain it wasn't a Native American disease. She didn't want people to think the disease only affected Navajo people. She also wanted to show that the Navajo people were strong. Hattie was able to interview tribal leaders and share stories about how their people were recovering from the illness.

Hattie didn't stop there. She wanted to share stories about Native American culture and people. Hattie found out that a Native American basketball team on a reservation had won 60 games in a row. Hattie featured the story on her show Good Morning America.

Hattie traveled around the world talking to presidents, astronauts, movie stars, and Olympians. But even so, Hattie's most memorable trip was traveling to a garbage dump in Mexico City, Mexico. In Mexico City, there were 30,000 people who did not have enough food and survived by scavenging the dump. It reminded Hattie of her childhood.

Hattie said, "It was the worst poverty I could imagine, and it changed my perspective on the poverty of my childhood. I asked a woman what was the most valuable thing she owned, and she said it was her family. It changed my life."

Hattie kept sharing stories that were truthful and respectful. More and more people listened. Hattie taught people about our common humanity. When people see how we are connected to each other, then people care. Hattie won four Emmy awards for her hard work.

Hattie inspires us *not to judge people* and instead learn their stories and get to know them.

SITTING BULL

Lakota Sioux
1831 - 1890

Sitting Bull dreamed of being a warrior. His father was a Lakota Sioux chief. His father was strong, brave, and a great warrior. Sitting Bull wanted to be just like him.

Sometimes that dream seemed impossible. People in his tribe did not think Sitting Bull was strong, brave, or a warrior. They thought he was slow. They even named him Slow. But he was just being careful and didn't like to rush.

When Slow was 10, he got a chance to show he could be a warrior. There was a buffalo hunt. Hundreds of buffalo were on the move, running fast. Slow's heart was beating fast too. But just like his name, he slowly and carefully chose a young buffalo and then killed it with two shots from his bow.

His father was proud. He was even prouder when Slow gave the buffalo to a family that needed food. Generosity was one of the most important Sioux values. Slow was on his way to becoming a warrior.

When Slow was 14, he got another chance to become a warrior. In Sioux culture, one of the bravest things that you could do was known as counting coup. Instead of shooting the enemy from afar, only the bravest would get really close to the enemy, tap the enemy with a special coup stick, and get away safely. It was the highest honor for the warriors.

Ten warriors from his tribe planned to attack the enemy. Slow didn't waste his chance, and he joined the warriors on their quest. For three days, they looked for their enemy. They found them camping by a creek. Slow and the warriors attacked. One of the enemies got on a horse. Slow chased him down, got his special coup stick, and used it to push the enemy off his horse. Slow had counted coup and shown he was a warrior!

His father was proud and gave him a party. His father also gave him a new name, Sitting Bull, because he was strong, patient, and a protector who would not back down.

Sitting Bull proved himself worthy of his new name. As he grew older, more white settlers entered the Sioux land, which included North Dakota and South Dakota. All the Sioux tribes were angry and had a meeting. They chose Sitting Bull to be the chief of chiefs, the leader of the entire Sioux nation. They believed Sitting Bull was strong and would protect them.

The U.S. government wanted Sitting Bull to sign a treaty. The treaty would force the Sioux to live on a reservation. Sitting Bull said no. He did not want to give up the Sioux way of life where they were free to go where they wanted.

Then, white miners found gold in the Black Hills. The Black Hills were a special place for the Sioux. Because of the gold discovery, white miners came from everywhere. The Sioux were angry. Sitting Bull called the tribes together to protect their land. The miners sought help from the U.S. government.

Sitting Bull and his people had bows and arrows. The U.S. government had guns. Even so, Sitting Bull and his people were strong and did not back down. The Sioux won.

The U.S. government could not believe they lost. They sent many troops and one by one, the chiefs surrendered. Sitting Bull moved his people to Canada. But there were not many buffalo, and his people grew hungry. Sitting Bull wanted to continue to fight, but he cared more about protecting his people. He returned to the U.S., with the last of the Sioux, to surrender.

Sitting Bull inspires us to *protect what we care about.* He teaches us to be strong and patient like a buffalo that holds his ground and never backs down.

RYNELDI BECENTI

Navajo
Born 1971

Ryneldi loved basketball. When she was a little girl, her dad gave her a blue and gold basketball. She carried the ball with her everywhere she went. She even slept with it!

Ryneldi would wake up early and start playing. There were no courts on their Navajo reservation in Arizona. So, her dad made a basketball court by sticking two poles into the ground fifty feet apart and attaching basketball hoops to each pole. Ryneldi would play in all kinds of weather – rain, wind, and snow. She would play day and night under the sun and moon.

Her mom cheered her on and told her to dream big. Ryneldi dreamed of being on a professional women's basketball team. There were no Native Americans or people who looked like her on teams like that. Ryneldi wanted to be the first.

When Ryneldi was in eighth grade, her mom died of cancer. Ryneldi was so sad, she wanted to quit. Her mom had been her biggest cheerleader. Ryneldi couldn't imagine playing without her mom cheering her on. But she remembered her mom's faith in her. Ryneldi's dream to be the first wasn't just for her. It was for her mom too. So Ryneldi kept going.

Her dad had his own ways to help Ryneldi train. He would drive slowly in his pick-up truck and yell at Ryneldi to pick up the bottles littered on the side of the road. Hours of this taught her how to be fast, make quick turns, and toss – all at the same time. This came in handy on the courts. Her ball-handling and sharp-shooting got better, and Ryneldi became the best at her high school, carrying her team to the state championship.

Ryneldi began her college basketball career at Scottsdale Community College in Phoenix. As much as she loved to play, Ryneldi was homesick. She missed life on the reservation. She missed her friends. She wanted to quit. But she remembered her mom and her dream to be the first. So, she kept going.

Ryneldi continued to practice in ways she'd learned from her dad. She would watch tapes of her favorite players and then spend hours on the court imitating their moves. Her favorite player was University of Southern California's star Cheryl Miller, one of the most famous woman basketball players. Cheryl could shoot, defend, rebound, and even dunk. Cheryl was African American, and it meant a lot to Ryneldi to see a woman of color out on the court. If Cheryl could do it, maybe Ryneldi could too.

Ryneldi's skills got even better. She scored over 2,000 points and was named Player of the Year. Arizona State University soon recruited Ryneldi. Native Americans from everywhere came to see her play. Some traveled for five hours. They wanted to support her. They wanted to see someone like them on the court.

Ryneldi amazed everyone and was an All-Pac 10 First Team selection in both her seasons at Arizona State University. She was also a two-time honorable mention All-America honoree.

After college, Ryneldi signed with the Phoenix Mercury, a professional women's basketball team. Her dream came true. She became the first Native American in the Women's NBA.

Even after all of her achievements, Ryneldi never forgot others. She wanted to help other Native Americans like her. Ryneldi went back home to her reservation. She set up free camps for many kids.

Ryneldi shows us that when something sad and hard happens to us, we can still keep moving forward to our dream. She inspires us to *remember our way and never give up.*

ALLAN HOUSER

Chiricahua Apache
1914 - 1994

Allan's father would tell him stories about their cousin Geronimo, the legendary Apache leader. Geronimo bravely led their Apache people against the U.S. government to keep their language and culture free and their own.

Allan loved these stories and was proud of his Apache culture. The more stories Allan heard, the more he wanted to write them down on paper. But he wasn't very good with words. He was better with drawing. So drawing became his way to share stories. Through his drawings, he would tell stories about his family and the history of his culture. He would draw day and night, even sneaking paper out of school and drawing on bars of soap – which made his mom mad!

Allan's family did not have much money, especially not for art classes, so Allan taught himself. One day, he saw a notice for an art school with a famous teacher. Allan applied and got into the Painting School at the Santa Fe Indian School. While he liked school, he thought that what they taught was too old-style. He wanted to try something new, something no one had ever seen before. And he didn't want to just do one type of art. He wanted to try all kinds of art and all kinds of styles. But his teacher told him no.

Allan left the school and tried new things. He tried watercolors. He tried wood carvings. He even tried full-sized paintings. He was chosen to paint life-sized murals in the Department of the Interior's building in Washington D.C. He painted three "Apache Scenes" called "Singing Love Songs," "Apache Round Dance," and "Sacred Fire Dance." People loved his work. He got to present his work all over the country, including the New York World's Fair in 1939.

One day, Allan saw a competition to design a sculpture for Native Americans who had served in World War II. The judges wanted people who knew how to sculpt. Allan did not know how to sculpt, but he decided to enter anyway.

Allan wanted to tell the world a story that honored Native Americans. He designed a 7-foot-tall statue of marble of a Native American wrapped in a shawl, a headdress by his feet. He called it "Comrade in Mourning." Many people entered the competition, but Allan won!

Allan taught himself how to sculpt. Allan found that when he sculpted, his heart sang. He had found the best way to tell stories from his heart.

Allan kept trying new things. He created sculptures in stone, wood, steel, and bronze to honor his people. He became famous throughout the world. In 1992, Allan was the first Native American to be awarded the National Medal of Arts by President George H. W. Bush.

Even though Allan was famous, he stayed humble. He wanted other Native Americans to have the chance to be artists. He remembered how as a child, he did not have money for art classes. So he became a teacher at a Native American school and taught many children that they could be artists too.

Allan shows us the power of art to connect to people's hearts. He inspires us to *try new things* and create something no one has seen before.

SUSAN LA FLESCHE PICOTTE

Omaha
1865 - 1915

When Susan was eight, she stayed at the bedside of a fellow Omaha Native woman who was very sick. They kept calling the white doctor for help. Each time, the doctor promised he would come. Each time, he didn't. They waited all through the night, but he never came.

Susan was sad that the white doctor did not value Native Americans. That night, Susan decided she would be a doctor. She would treat all patients, no matter who they were.

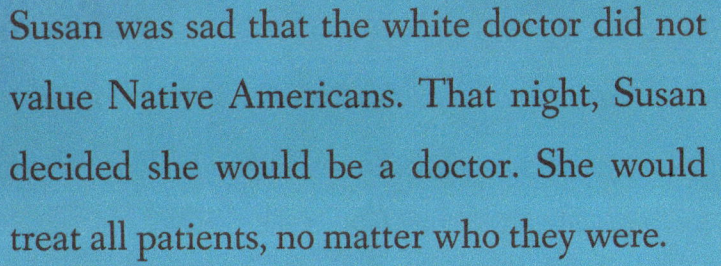

Her dream was not easy. She needed courage to travel far away to school. She left her Omaha Reservation in Nebraska to go to Hampton University on the east coast. She missed her family and friends. But Susan focused on her dream. She graduated second in her class.

Susan couldn't stop there. To be a doctor, Susan needed to go to medical school. But in the 1880s, there were not many women in medical school, let alone Native Americans. Susan also did not have the money to go to school. But she didn't give up. Other women doctors noticed how hard Susan worked, and they helped her get a scholarship. Susan attended Woman's Medical College of Pennsylvania. She graduated at the top of her class! In 1889, she became Doctor Sue, the first Native American woman doctor.

Susan was excited to go back to her Omaha reservation in Nebraska. But back home, her Omaha people did not trust her. They were used to white doctors. They were used to men.

Susan did not give up. She treated her first Native American patient, a young boy. His family was amazed when the boy got better quickly, and they shared the news with their friends. Soon, many Native Americans came to get Susan's help. She was the only doctor for more than a thousand people spread over a territory about the size of Rhode Island.

Susan traveled to help sick people. Even before the sun rose, Susan would get up and put on her buffalo robe. She would ride her horse through the wind and snow – sometimes 50 miles or more – to care for someone who was sick. She would help patients even if they could not pay and used her own money to buy supplies. Susan kept working hard and opened a hospital in her hometown. The hospital was for everyone who needed help. Susan's dream had come true.

Susan teaches us that caring for our community takes courage – like courage to be the first woman doctor and courage to be rejected by the very people we are trying to serve. She inspires us that when we face hard times to *focus on our love for our community.*

JASON BALDES

Eastern Shoshone
Born 1978

Growing up in the Wind River Reservation in Wyoming, Jason loved to spend time with his dad. His dad was a biologist with the U.S. Fish and Wildlife Service. Together, they would ride horses and collect water from the lakes and rivers to make sure the water was healthy.

Along the way, his dad would point out the plants and animals and share how important they were to Native Americans. Plants and animals took care of Native Americans, and Native Americans in return took care of the plants and animals.

When Jason was 18, he went on the trip of a lifetime with his dad to Africa. There, Jason got to see wild animals like elephants, giraffes, and lions. Most magical of all were the wildebeests. One and a half million of them moved together across the Serengeti in Tanzania and the Masai Mara plains in Kenya.

Jason was amazed to see so many animals together on their great migration. He was even more amazed when his dad told him that this enormous herd of wildebeests was nothing compared to the number of buffalo that used to roam in America 200 years ago.

When Jason and his dad returned to America, Jason wanted to learn as much as possible about the American buffalo. He learned that buffalo were very important to the Native Americans. Buffalo provided food, clothes, tools, fuel, and homes. Native Americans respected buffalo and only killed what they needed. Jason was sad to learn that the U.S. government had wanted to get rid of the Native Americans, and so they purposefully destroyed their buffalo food source. The once vast herds of over 30 million buffalo were killed until only 541 were left.

Jason went to Montana State University to study more. But it wasn't easy. He had a family with four kids. It was hard to find the money and time for both his family and for school. Jason almost gave up. But he had an important goal. He wanted to bring the buffalo back to their original homeland.

Jason worked hard and learned more about how to bring the buffalo back. It took 10 years for Jason to finish school.

As soon as he finished, Jason began to make his dream come true. He looked for pure buffalo. He talked to his tribe, the community, and nature groups about why it was important to bring the buffalo back. He found land where the buffalo could roam wild. He researched ways the community could learn from the buffalo and connect with their Native American history.

After years of hard work, in 2016, Jason was able to bring 10 buffalo back to the Wind River Reservation in Wyoming. It was the first time the buffalo had roamed these lands since 1885.

Jason is partnering with Native Americans and non-Native Americans to bring more buffalo back to the Wind River Reservation and have them roam free. Together, they are bringing more animals back to the Wind River Reservation – not just buffalo but grizzly bear, wolves, moose, deer, elk, and bighorn sheep.

Jason teaches us that we are connected to nature. He inspires us to *take care of animals and plants*, just as they take care of us.

MARIA TALLCHIEF

Osage

1925 - 2013

As a girl, Maria loved her tribe's dances. She loved the music, singing, and dancing. In her Osage culture, this was how they told stories. Maria wanted to become a dancer.

During the week, Maria took ballet classes. During the weekends, she performed at county fairs and rodeos. Maria would dance ballet to "Stars and Stripes Forever" with an American flag sewn into her cape.

When Maria was eight, her family moved from Oklahoma to Los Angeles so she could dance on bigger stages. But in Los Angeles, Maria felt like an outsider. The kids asked why she didn't wear feathers in her hair. They made battle cries when they saw her. They made fun of her name. They asked her if she was tall or if she was a chief. Maria decided to combine her last name to Tallchief to help her be more accepted.

Dancing helped Maria feel better. With each twirl and leap, her heart would fill with happiness.

One day, there was an audition for Maria's favorite ballet, the Chopin Concerto. She thought she was perfect for the top ballerina spot. Maria practiced even more. Her teacher said, "When you sleep, sleep like a ballerina. On the street waiting for a bus, stand like a ballerina." At the audition, Maria performed her best. She thought she would be picked.

Maria did not get picked. Instead, she was given the part of a background dancer. She was devastated. She stopped working hard. Her mom told her, "You have to show that you want to dance with all your heart."

So, Maria put her heart into dancing. She never took her eyes off the teacher, even when she was helping a classmate. Outside of class, Maria would repeat the steps in her head. Her teacher noticed and spent extra time helping Maria. Maria got better and better.

Maria went to New York City to try out for a famous ballet company called the Ballet Russe. At first, they told her that they didn't need any more dancers. Maria burst into tears. She had taken a train a long way for this one chance to make her dream come true. But Maria had a lucky break. One of the dancers left unexpectedly, and they had an open spot. The leader remembered Maria from his visit to Los Angeles. He remembered her strength, focus, and grace. He decided to offer Maria the spot.

Maria was now in Ballet Russe, one of the best ballet companies in the world. She felt scared to be around such talented ballerinas. Most of them were Russian. They told her to change her name so that it sounded more Russian, then she could get more respect. Maria did not want to change her name. She was a proud Native American.

Maria kept giving her all during rehearsals and added more practice sessions. The leader noticed. He picked her to be the back-up for the top ballerina. People told him this was a mistake. Maria was too young and did not have enough experience. Maria kept her focus. She watched the more experienced dancers to learn more and got even better.

One day, the top ballerina was sick. It was time for Maria to be in the spotlight. Maria was nervous. She did not think she could do it. When the curtains rose, she took a deep breath. She leaped, twirled, and soared. The next day, the newspapers said that she danced like a bird. But they focused more on her being a Native American instead of how well she danced. Maria wanted to show the world that Native Americans could be the best at anything.

Maria got even more precise with her craft, learning how to hold her chest higher, keep her back straighter, and keep her feet arched longer. Maria got better and better. Maria got picked for her dream job at last. She became a prima ballerina, the top job in the company. This company had never picked an American, let alone a Native American. Maria didn't waste her chance. She kept giving her all in practices and performances. She was the star of many shows including *Swan Lake* and *The Firebird*. Maria's dream had come true!

Maria inspires us to *work hard with all of our heart*. She shows us that we can be the best if we try our best.

CHESTER NEZ

Navajo
1921 — 2014

Chester grew up on a farm on a Navajo reservation in New Mexico. Together, Chester and his family would herd sheep, plant corn, and harvest the crops. Even his neighbors would come to help. They all worked together as one. It was the Navajo way.

When Chester was eight, he had to leave for boarding school. This was common for Native American children as there were no schools close to their homes. Families had to send their child to a school many miles away. The families had no idea that these schools were part of the U.S. government's plan to erase their culture.

Chester was sad to leave his family and Navajo culture behind. At boarding school, they cut his hair, made him wear a uniform, and told him not to speak his language. Any student caught speaking their language would get beaten or have their mouth washed out with soap.

When Chester was in tenth grade, Japan attacked Pearl Harbor, a U.S. military base in Hawaii. President Roosevelt declared war. Before this declaration, the U.S. and the Navajo had fought each other. But now, the U.S. wanted the Navajos' help. Chester wanted to defend his country. He felt that America had always been his land, even before the white people came. Chester wanted to show that the U.S. and Navajos could work together as one.

Chester joined the military. He was glad that he never forgot his Navajo language. The language that the government had tried to destroy was the language that the U.S. now needed to win the war. Navajo was a special language that only Navajos could speak. There were special sounds that only someone born to the language knew. The U.S. needed an unbreakable code if they wanted to beat the enemy. They found that code in the Navajo language.

Chester and the other 28 Navajos became code talkers. A code talker could speak in a code, a secret language that they hoped the enemy would not understand. The problem was that the Japanese were very good at breaking American codes. But Chester and the other code talkers worked together to create a new code that the Japanese couldn't break.

To create the new code, the code talkers took each letter of the English alphabet and picked an English word that started with that letter. Then they translated that English word into a Navajo word.

They created a code alphabet.

"A." Ant. *Wol-la-chee*.

"B." Bear. *Shush*.

"C." Cat. *Moasi*.

"D." Deer. *Be*.

So, the word "bad," B-A-D would be *Shush — Wol-la-chee — Be*.

It had to be perfect. Even one syllable that was not perfect could mess up the code. After training for many weeks, they were ready to put the new code into action.

Chester and his partner rode the USS *Lurline* ship to the Guadalcanal island in the South Pacific. When they got there, Chester and his partner dug a hole to hide in. With bullets flying, this was their main way to protect themselves.

With their hearts pounding, they got ready for their first message. Once it arrived, Chester and his partner translated it using their Navajo code. They sent the message over the radio to the other partners far away. Now they all could talk to each other and know what was going on. They were working together as one.

The Japanese could not understand the new code. Chester and the other code talkers sent many codes over many months. Because of the code talkers, the U.S. was able to beat the enemy.

After the war, the code talkers were told to keep their code a secret. It wasn't until 25 years later that the truth was shared. Chester and the code talkers were given Congressional Gold Medals by President George W. Bush.

Chester and the code talkers inspire us to *work together as one*. They teach us the power of teamwork and that we are stronger together.

MARY GOLDA ROSS

Cherokee
1908 - 2008

Mary was good at math. People thought math was for boys not girls. So, when Mary was in the higher math classes, she was often the only girl there. But Mary didn't mind. She was Cherokee. In her culture, school and math were for everyone—boys and girls.

Mary also didn't mind because she had other things to think about. Like space travel. She would look at the night sky and dream of what it was like to travel in space. In the 1920s, that dream seemed impossible. No one had ever traveled in space before.

When Mary went to Northeastern State Teachers College in Oklahoma, she continued to focus on what she loved—math. Again, she was the only woman, and her male classmates would often sit on the opposite side of the classroom. But Mary didn't mind. She worked extra hard to get better grades than them.

Back then, the only jobs available to women were jobs like teaching and nursing. After she graduated, Mary decided to teach. She liked her job, and she loved her students. But she never stopped dreaming about space travel.

The U.S. was entering World War II, and her dad suggested that Mary could use her math to help. Back then, there were no computers. They needed humans to do math. They were hiring women to do these jobs. Mary was excited. This was her chance!

Mary applied and got the job at Lockheed Aerospace Corporation. She was so good at her job that the company's leaders noticed her. They asked if she wanted to be an engineer. She would get the chance to do more math. Mary said yes. She went to the University of California, Los Angeles to learn how to create aircraft and rockets. Afterwards, she became an aerospace engineer. She was going to design rockets that would bring astronauts into space. Her dream was coming true!

In 1952, Mary was invited to a special team of 40 engineers. They were the best of the best. They were a top secret group to create rockets the world had never seen before. Mary was the only woman and the only Native American. She didn't mind. She remembered her Cherokee value that men and women were equal. She was just as good.

It was an exciting time. America was in a great space race. America was racing to be the first country to put a human on the moon. Mary and her team worked hard. In 1969, when an American was the first to land on the moon, Mary was proud that she as a Cherokee woman helped make that happen.

Mary was the first Native American woman engineer and one of the first women rocket scientists. After her career, she gave talks to high school and college students to encourage young women and Native Americans to study math and science and become engineers.

Mary teaches us that men and women are equal. She shows us that *women can do anything they dream of*. Education is power, and when women get an education, they can change the world.

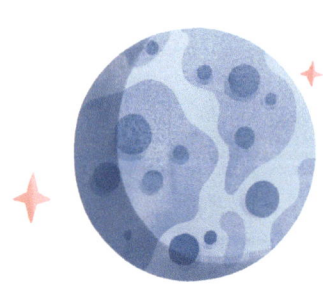

COCHISE

Chiricahua Apache
1810 - 1874

Cochise's dad was a great chief. His dad taught him to be a warrior, shooting arrows and riding a horse bareback a hundred miles in one day. His dad taught him to be like an antelope, running miles and miles on the hot and harsh desert sand without food or water.

His dad taught him to hear like an owl, noticing the sounds of fox barks and coyote cries. Most importantly, his dad taught him to be a leader, practicing the Apache value of always telling the truth.

When Cochise got older, he became the leader of his tribe. Cochise wanted to be the best leader for his people. He remembered what his dad had taught him and was always honest. Even when it was hard, he never lied. His people grew to trust him.

Where Cochise lived, he'd only seen Native Americans. Native Americans shared the land equally amongst themselves. Now as a chief, he became worried as more and more white settlers took land. The white settlers declared that the land was theirs and the Native Americans needed to stay out. Cochise wanted to have peace with the white settlers. He wanted to trust them and for them to trust him, so he met with them, and they agreed to be at peace.

All was peaceful for five years until one day in 1861. A white settler's farm was attacked, and a child was kidnapped. The leader of the white settlers thought that it was Cochise's people who had attacked. Cochise told him the truth. It was not his tribe. The settlers did not believe Cochise, and so a war began.

Cochise still wanted peace and wanted to build trust with the white settlers and their leader. The leader invited Cochise and his family to dinner in his tent. Cochise believed the leader was being honest and brought his family. Cochise was shocked when the leader took his family and him hostage so that the kidnapped child would be returned. Cochise cut a hole in the tent and escaped, but his family was trapped.

The war continued. Cochise still wanted peace and knew that this was only possible if the settlers and Apaches could trust each other. Cochise met with a general of the white settlers. Cochise told the general the truth that he had not attacked the white settler's farm. Cochise also spent time with the general so that they could build trust. He showed the general the Chiricahua Mountains and shared why they were sacred to his tribe. He invited the general to meet his family and shared stories of their people. The general began to trust Cochise, and they agreed to stop fighting. The war came to an end and peaceful times were ahead.

Cochise inspires us to *be honest*, even when it is hard. He shows us that peace is possible by telling the truth and trusting each other.

ZITKALA-SA

Yankton Dakota Sioux
1876 - 1938

Gertrude Simmons did not get her name from her parents. She got her name from the white settlers. The white settlers wanted Gertrude to be more like them instead of her Yankton Dakota Sioux people.

Although Gertrude had a white settler's name, she had a Sioux heart. As a girl, Gertrude loved sitting with her Sioux tribe around a fire listening to stories. Listening to these old stories passed down over many generations, Gertrude knew that she had to keep these stories alive.

As much as she loved the Sioux stories, Gertrude was curious about stories from outside of her Yankton Dakota Sioux tribe in South Dakota. Her brother told her stories about his boarding school far away in Indiana. Students could ride a train that was like an iron horse to the school and eat delicious apples. Gertrude thought the school sounded magical and wanted to go too.

When she arrived at the school, Gertrude soon found that the school wasn't magical at all. She missed her friends. She could only speak English. Worst of all, she was forced to get her hair cut. Gertrude tried to hide under a bed. But they found her, tied her to a chair, and cut her braids. Gertrude cried. She felt like the school was trying to erase everything that was important to her.

There was one thing that she loved about school. She learned to read and write. Writing stories was a way to keep her culture alive.

She gave herself the new name Zitkala-Sa. This means Red Bird. With her new name, Zitkala-Sa wanted to use her voice like a bird sharing stories about her people.

As a student at Earlham College, Zitkala-Sa entered a speech contest. Most of the crowd was white. People were not used to seeing a Native American, let alone a woman who was a writer too. People made fun of her. They hung a big banner with a drawing of a pitiful Native American girl who looked like she was about to cry.

When it was her turn to speak, Zitkala-Sa was nervous. She took a deep breath. She reminded herself why she was doing this. Zitkala-Sa spoke passionately from her heart. She forgot the crowd. She shared her speech, "Side by Side," and what it felt like for Native Americans to be treated as lower than white people. She shared how Native Americans and white people have a common humanity and that Native Americans should be treated as equals. After her speech, the crowd clapped and cheered. They took down the sign. Zitkala-Sa won second place!

Zitkala-Sa wanted to share more stories. Most people did not know much about Native Americans. She wanted to share stories like the ones that she heard when she sat with her people around the fire. She wanted to share about Native American values of generosity and kindness and their respect for nature and animals. She wanted to share why it was not fair to have their land taken away. She wanted to share how schools should not erase Native American culture.

Because of her, people paid attention and wanted to help. In 1924, Zitkala-Sa helped create the Indian Citizenship Act so that Native Americans could become American citizens. She also helped create the Indian Reorganization Act that gave Native Americans more freedom to make decisions for themselves instead of having the U.S. government decide for them. Zitkala-Sa also helped create the National Council of American Indians so that Native Americans from different tribes could work together and champion Native American rights.

Zitkala-Sa inspires us to *reclaim who we are and use our voice* to share our stories. She teaches us that stories can bring people together to do what is right.

How will **YOU** change the world?

Draw your own portrait.

Name: _____

Further Reading

Jason Baldes
Admin. "Jason Baldes, Eastern Shoshone, Wind River Native Advocacy Center, Executive Director." *Winds of Change*, 22 Jan. 2015, woc.aises.org/content/jason-baldes-eastern-shoshone-wind-river-native-advocacy-center-executive-director.

Ryneldi Becenti
Marshall, John. "Arizona State Retires Ryneldi Becenti's Number." *Spokesman.com*, The Spokesman-Review, 25 Dec. 2013, www.spokesman.com/stories/2013/dec/26/arizona-state-retires-ryneldi-becentis-number/.

Cochise
Sweeney, Edwin R. Cochise: *Chiricahua Apache Chief*. University of Oklahoma Press, 1995.

John Herrington
Herrington, John B. *Mission to Space*. White Dog Press, 2016.

Allan Houser
Perlman, Barbara H., and Allan Houser. Allan Houser. *Smithsonian Institute PR*, 1992.

Hattie Kauffman
Kauffman, Hattie. *Falling into Place: a Memoir of Overcoming*. Baker Books, a Division of Baker Publishing Group, 2014.

Wilma Mankiller
Mankiller, Wilma Pearl, and Michael Wallis. *Mankiller a Chief and Her People*. St. Martin's Griffin, 2000.

Chester Nez
Nez, Chester, et al. *Code Talker: the First and Only Memoir by One of the Original Navajo Code Talkers of WWII*. Berkley Caliber, 2012.

Elizabeth Peratrovich
Boochever, Annie. *Fighter in Velvet Gloves: Alaska Civil Rights Hero Elizabeth Peratrovich*. University of Alaska Press, 2019.

Susan La Flesche Picotte
Starita, Joe. *Warrior of the People: How Susan La Flesche Overcame Racial and Gender Inequality to Become America's First Indian Doctor*. St. Martin's Press, 2016.

Mary Golda Ross
Brewer, Graham. "Rocket Woman." Oklahomatoday.com, 2018.

Wes Studi
Murg, Wilhelm. "Cover Story: Oklahoma Actor Wes Studi Blazes Trail for Native Filmmakers, Actors and Civil Rights." *Oklahoma Gazette*, Oklahoma Gazette, 28 Jan. 2021, www.okgazette.com/oklahoma/cover-story-oklahoma-actor-wes-studi-blazes-trail-for-native-filmmakers-actors-and-civil-rights/Content?oid=2957948.

Maria Tallchief
Tallchief, Maria. *Tallchief America's Prima Ballerina*. Paw Prints, 2009.

Jim Thorpe
Wheeler, Robert W. *Jim Thorpe, World's Greatest Athlete*. University of Oklahoma Press, 1979.

Sitting Bull
LaPointe, Ernie. *Sitting Bull: His Life and Legacy*. Gibbs M Smith Inc, 2021.

Zitkala-Sa
Lewandowski, Tadeusz. *Red Bird, Red Power: The Life and Legacy of Zitkala-Ša (Volume 67)*. University of Oklahoma Press, 2019.

Thank you

for reading our book!

If would mean the world to us if you could take a short minute to leave a review on Amazon, as your kind feedback is much appreciated. Please go to *amazon.com/author/analiza*. Click on the book, scroll down, and click "Write a customer review."

Thank you very much for your time!

—*Analiza and Bryson*

To Scarlet and Bryson for inspiring me to be brave — AQW

To Mommy, Daddy, and Scarlet for all of our fun adventures — BQW

Text & illustration copyright 2022 by Analiza Quiroz Wolf

Cover & illustration by Andreea Chele

All rights reserved. No part of this publication may be reproduced, stored in a retrieval system, or transmitted in any form or by any means, without the prior written permission of the publisher/author. For information regarding permission, write to analiza@analizawolf.com.

Website: https://analizawolf.com/books

Wishful Wolf Press
ISBN Soft Cover: 979-8-9861183-1-4
ISBN Hard Cover: 979-8-9861183-2-1

Lightning Source UK Ltd.
Milton Keynes UK
UKHW051145240522
403421UK00002B/41